Volume 91 of the Yale Series of Younger Poets

CITIES OF MEMORY

Ellen Hinsey

Foreword by James Dickey

Yale University Press   New Haven & London

Published with the assistance of a gift from The Guinzberg Fund and a grant to honor James Merrill.

Set in Janson Text type by Keystone Typesetting, Inc., Orwigsburg, Pennsylvania. Printed in the United States of America by Thomson-Shore, Inc., Dexter, Michigan.

Library of Congress Cataloging-in-Publication Data
Hinsey, Ellen, 1960–
    Cities of memory / Ellen Hinsey ; foreword by James Dickey.
      p.   cm. — (Yale series of younger poets ; v. 91)
    ISBN 0-300-06673-2 (cloth : alk. paper). —
  ISBN 0-300-06674-0 (pbk. : alk. paper)
     I. Title. II. Series.
    PS3558.I5469C58 1996
    811'.54—dc20   95-51388
                              CIP

A catalogue record for this book is available from the British Library.

10 9 8 7 6 5 4 3 2 1

Ihr naht euch wieder, schwankende Gestalten,
Die früh sich einst dem trüben Blick gezeigt.
Versuch ich wohl, euch diesmal festzuhalten?

Once more, dim wavering figures from the past,
You come, who once rose to my troubled eyes.
Shall I attempt this time to hold you fast?

Goethe, *Faust* 1–3
(translated by Charles E. Passage)

CONTENTS

Foreword by James Dickey   ix

Acknowledgments   xiii

Part I/Cities of Memory

March 26, 1827   3

The Approach of War   6

Lebensraum   7

The Disasters of War, Spain, 1810   11

Return of the Partisan's Son   12

Trieste   15

Trains at Night   16

Part II/The Art of Measuring Light

The Art of Measuring Light   21

The Body in Youth   23

Diptych   25

    I. Pietà   25

    II. Arranging the Garments   26

Parable of the Lovers   27

On a Visit to Budapest   29

Fantasie on *The Church at Auvers*   30

Part III/The Jumping Figure

The Stairwell, Berggasse 19, Vienna   35

Night in Clamart   39

From: *The Seven Wonders of the Modern World*   41

The Roman Arbor   43

Planisféria, Map of the World, Lisbon, 1554   45

Death of the Tyrant   46

The Jumping Figure   48

Part IV/The Idiom of the Place

Paula Modersohn-Becker at Worpswede   53

Munch in Oslo   55

Reading   57

Waking at Night   58

Photograph, Off the Dry Salvages   60

The Sermon to Fishes   61

Tones Overheard on Monastery Grounds   62

Canticle in Grey   64

Notes   67

FOREWORD

The need for roots, as Simone Weil reminds us, is fundamental to human kind; there is no one wearing our shape who has not felt it. But, along with this condition, there are those who can take root in places where they do not expect to live out the rest of their lives and die. To an American from Massachusetts there is in Italy

> *in an alcove of green, the quick movement*
> *of a lizard as it traced the sandal*
> *of a departed goddess.*

or in Budapest she finds that

> *One cannot live without love — this statement*
> *so simple, so mundane, came to me in that*
> *city where we roamed around the baths.*

There are many such sensibilities, and they are almost without exception given to people combining a powerful, empathetic imagination, a sense of adventure and exploration, a quickness at learning languages not native to them, and a very strong desire for spiritual quest in locations that they either seek out or have thrust upon them by circumstances.

> *The moon is seldom full. In Trieste, Joyce still walks,*
> *an impassioned man, bearing his one good eye.*
> *The shore beats back its own pulse.*
> *Roofs sigh. Men hitch up their pants,*
> *leave without a sound.*

> *Night hoists its bags and continues, there is always a later train.*

In a good many instances these poets — they are always poets whether they write or not — are set going by the experience of language itself; they want to read and speak as though words new to them were equivalents of other psychic dimensions.

Though it should be obvious that Ellen Hinsey has not spent months or years in all of these "Cities of Memory" and has probably visited some of them briefly, or only in her imagination, it ought to be equally plain that for the creative beholder, the true artist, a little time is enough, the mind is enough. In these encounters one is privileged to experience surroundings as though they were not observations but visions, for all poets are embarked on Coleridge's ship, invented from a sea which the writer has never actually felt rise and fall.

Empathy — though the German word *Einfühlung* is stronger — constitutes one of the poet's primary tools. Like any attitude or device, it can be overused and misused, resulting in Ruskin's familiar Pathetic Fallacy, examples of which are among the true horrors of literature, suspending belief at a touch. Yet the greatest writers employ it extensively, and some, like Rilke, would be lost without it. And thus it is true that one comes with a sense of relief and rightness on Aldous Huxley's characterization of D. H. Lawrence; we need his capacities:

> *He seemed to know, by personal experience, what it was like to be a tree or a daisy or a breaking wave or even the mysterious moon itself. He could get inside the skin of an animal and tell how, dimly, inhumanly, it thought.*

Ms. Hinsey's empathy runs to cultures, their people and artifacts, rather than to the things of nature. Fountains, streets, trains — especially apt for her purposes — portraits — refugees, artists, and other survivors — are quietly, passionately felt, exactly limned, washed in clear grey.

Artists; yes. A great many poets are moved to write about works of art and their makers, arts other than their own, but not many are successful. Yet when the right poet and subject of this kind come together, the results can be unique, adding dimensions to both disciplines. Hinsey's poem on Modersohn-Becker at Worpswede, an artists' haven which at the same time included the young Rilke, then on his way to becoming the very emperor of *Einfühlung*, is to my mind the best rendering of one art by means of another since Proust's evocation of Elstir's canal-webbed town, with its houses and ships interacting, exchanging identities:

> *Each morning, from the same palette*
> *the landlocked hamlet came to light.*
> *Night had sketched the shadowy forms,*
> *and from its traces, birches, brave white,*
>
> *issued forth their lines, laced the canal's*
> *sinuous path. You began here: this marsh*
> *the ground of your colors; you faced*
> *the unlanguagable green of firs, drew*
>
> *the uncombed bank alight. Evening saw*
> *your reflection bend in the paleness*
> *at the water's edge, and pass where piled*
> *peat rose, darkened like temples after*
>
> *sudden rain. You loved the idiom*
> *of the place.*

With her quiet and deep involvement in other places and tongues, her true-running imagination, Ellen Hinsey comes to rest in many ways and places, from her own United States to France, Italy, Germany, Spain, Hungary, Austria, Russia, and Norway. Though not native-born to these, she is at the center of them just the same, by virtue and talent one of the best kinds of human being: the perceptive voyager, the sympathetic and vivid stranger.

ACKNOWLEDGMENTS

Acknowledgment is made to the following journals and anthologies
for poems which first appeared in them or are forthcoming:

Fear and the Muse:	"Canticle in Grey"
(Zebra Consortium)	
The Missouri Review:	"The Approach of War"
	"The Disasters of War, Spain, 1810"
	"On a Visit to Budapest"
	"Night in Clamart"
	"The Roman Arbor"
	"Death of the Tyrant"
	"The Jumping Figure"
The New England Review:	"Photograph, Off the Dry Salvages"
The Paris Review:	"The Sermon to Fishes"
The Southern Poetry Review:	"*Planisféria*, Map of the World, Lisbon, 1554"
	"From: *The Seven Wonders of the Modern World*"
The Spoon River Poetry Review:	"The Art of Measuring Light"

Grateful acknowledgment is made to the following for permission to
quote material in copyright:

Princeton University Press: excerpts from "The Crisis of the Mind"
by Paul Valéry, in *History and Politics* © 1962, translated by Denise
Folliot and Jackson Mathews.

Prentice-Hall Inc., Upper Saddle River, NJ 07458: excerpts from Michael Grant's *History of Rome* © 1978, p. 5.

Acknowledgment is given to those individuals who gave valuable criticism during the formative stages of the manuscript: Mark Carlson, Ann Owens, Terry Pollack, Dale Roche, Alice van Buren, Kathleen Spivack, and D. M. Thomas.

Special thanks are also given to my extended family in the United States and France — *à ceux qui ont vu tant d'étoiles et tant de terres dépassées.*

I

Cities of Memory

We had long heard tell of whole worlds that had
vanished, of empires sunk without a trace, gone
down with all their machines into the unexplor-
able depths of the centuries . . . but the disasters
that had sent them down were, after all, none of
our affair.

We see now that the abyss of history is deep
enough to hold us all.

Paul Valéry, *The Crisis of the Mind*

MARCH 26, 1827

Plaudite amici, comœdia finita est!

Beethoven on his deathbed

I

In the room where the figure lay,
a damped ivory under time's
finger, agitated voices betrayed

their fear that, with his passing,
the last of sound would be carted off—
the price exacted in recompense.

They had to admit, in retrospect,
he had only ever been borrowed.
Now he was being taken back.

So when a voice outside displayed
the range of limited vocal flight
the exclamation was received

with relief. The body was watched.
In the final hour the pallid frame
offered to explain a thing or two

if only in the register of dreams:
Do you hear the tolling?
Change the scene! In an alley

of memory with light dimming,
the opera's curtain rose out of habit,
falling to the sound of trumpets.

II

That music is not the note
but the interval —
that it is not the note but
the possibility that lies between,

the sparrow in the field
and the silence after,
the approach of rain and the road's
washed shadow.

The world with eighty-eight
tones that wait to tell us of agony
and agony's lifting,
the done and left undone.

III

When over, all Vienna came,
Death had called them in their
best. So black-gloved with
lilies on their northern shoulders,

they followed dutifully the
funeral bier, four abreast.
The opera chorus, then the friars,
the conductors and the socialites.

Trombones sounded, but once
emitted, music sank to the soil,
as on the coldest days, when a shout
disappears quickly as vapor

dissolved in the air's oceanic vast.
Beyond, it was sound
that wept, and played a march
in the loved octaves,

knowing the future's empty
shape, seeing events and figures
in the angled glass — dark times
would henceforth call it back.

THE APPROACH OF WAR

That morning, daylight was the same.
        Everyday rituals, observed by no one,
    left the bedroom door open as a jaw in sleep.
   The faucet's three-four time went unnoticed.

At midday, a ragged curtain shifted in the breeze.
        The paper's checkered voice quietly yellowed.
   When afternoon arrived, there was soot in the air,
   and birds stayed nested in the dark, thatched groves.

Across an open field, a querulous voice called once
        and received its answer.
   The road was empty. A car, wrapped in dust,
   swept the lane, vanished.

The willows were still. A door mated a latch.
        At dusk the smell of pears rose,
   and a mist trawled the lake.
   A match was cupped under the dome of a palm.

Night, not yet soiled, made its way across
        the lake and into the arms of branches.

LEBENSRAUM

The Romans now felt ready to move against the Veii,
and they were all the more eager to do so because they
themselves . . . stood in urgent need of new land.

Michael Grant, *History of Rome*

I. Rome

In that place of marred beginnings,
                shaded by cypress and chestnut leaf,

ringed by hills whose seven vistas
                reached past the Tiber to the sea, there

encircled by roads, walls, marshes,
                in the center, two-doored, prescient,

lay the temple of Janus. In the web
                of evening's shadow, the dual face

watched both doors, as the young,
                their bodies strung like lyres, passed by

on their way to war. Janus, seer
                of future and past, foreseer of all

human folly, marked each breath
                as if the last, knowing how sword or

ash-carved bow might come to take
                the final note. But the empire would last:

the wolf-nursed offspring had not
　　　　　brought curse, but promise of a prosperous

birth, to lead the strong from close
　　　　　fertile lands to rock-strewn shores.

When dawn touched again the field,
　　　　　it saw horses wild on the grasses, and death

had crept deep into each carcass
　　　　　as the olive lizard enters the broken stone.

When the news of the dead was
　　　　　carried back, each gathered theirs like

goods from a cart, and returning
　　　　　to the familiar hearth, spread it beneath

the lamp of their private grief.
　　　　　When together the voices rose, a sorrow

thick as smoke hung above the houses,
　　　　　the city covered as with a terrible net,

and by the wind's syncopation, leaves
　　　　　framed and unframed the marble head.

II. Europe, 1938

Traffic pulsed under leaden skies,
                    at corners where crowds, paralyzed

by go or stop, waited for a sign
                    to turn them again to the daily task.

Beyond them, daylight wound its path —
                    pausing on bridges where taxis passed,

and below, on the cargo of rusted barges;
                    and entered, finally, a still-dark hall,

quiet beneath the marble of its dome.
                    Here the hopeful gathered, and opened

the door to sound. For somehow there
                    lingered the shape of a thought not

yet debased: *time still for the unity of
                    the forces,* long anticipated, long overdue.

For perhaps what had trained
            Beethoven's hand or had guided

the curve of Berlioz's thought could
            reign: each orchestra at the same

moment could warm its notes to the
            same verdant plain. Music could

hold forth in the curved gallery,
            raising for once its measured voice.

Above, the busts of the ancient scribes,
            that like an alphabet crown a hall,

ventured each a slow downward glance
            and watched, as the voices rose,

water flowing bleakly from the dark forests,
            standards rising in the eagle's shadow.

Beneath his long-weathered arbor, Janus
            opened the door of night, and watched

as those few hopeful fled — as any music that
            might have sounded fell to the grass

as the dew was drying under the hoofs
            of the fallen Polish cavalry.

THE DISASTERS OF WAR, SPAIN, 1810

After Goya

The fires were low, and because it was
    night, the engine of folly had taken
        to flight for a time. I walked the rows,
    roaming as one would a ruined place,

my lantern not Diogenes', but seeking
    a recognizable face among the carnage.
        My lamp swung low, a censer of light.
    I stopped, for a hand reached up, lit

for a moment in its dreaming. What
    my hand touched I didn't know — I
        pieced through bodies as a river goes,
    threading myself, as if around the rocks:

dark bodies lay like slate in that empty
    cleft of night. All the world's passion
        spent, left to rot on the ground. Day alone
    would see me fallen. There perhaps I

lay with you, as only my empty lantern
    knew, casting its last flame on your back,
        your hands entwined, your jaw gone slack —
    praying face down in the mud.

                Para eso habéis nacido.
                    (For this you were born.)

RETURN OF THE PARTISAN'S SON

The train led us past homeland bleakly scarred,
    then day left us, and we went on in darkness —
Beyond, the city was divided: open to those who
    knew its worth — by virtue of blood or birth,
we plunged on towards it. On our retinas would
    remain the charge of hamlets sighted,
burnt to char, and soldiers settled as locusts will.
    Our arrival was cautious and without reception.
Though on entering where doves and passengers wait,
    the door, as if cognizant, registered opposition.
The clock retreated before advancing.

Each detail now seemed to hang in the balance,
    distorted as a specimen held under glass:
we imagined in each face a prior knowledge,
    and each word a lorry of hidden suspicion.
Yet our primary witness in that midnight hour
    viewed us from his own enclosure: behind
the grill he trod skeptical and predatory, like
    an animal that has mastered its requisite prison.
Our eyes met and locked, but the message was
    strange: for whose is the greater loss —
the hand and head tethered to a city's betrayal,
    or the exile condemned to beg news from a stone?

The city lay before us like a darkened crown,
    and we could grieve its once-treasured work:
chimneys, bridges, blackened spires —
    an abbey's open vaults and the altar's fire.

The hour's sharp edge separated present and past.
　　And indeed, what of the days spent waiting?
the moments that weighed like sand in a glove —
　　And who, now, the figure lost thinking,
caught up in possible but unimaginable acts?
　　Now when all was done, confessed —
now when the road and night's dark brow
　　seemed frightening as the spirit manifest.

Yet further on, where a yellow lamp burned,
　　we found faces familiar for their cast,
and night divulged its store of reasons —
　　I have partisan's blood in me, the sum of days
spent in the shadow of my father's exile.
　　There, he lived consonant and species bound,
fastened on the cataloging of remembered
　　things: the bird that will not sing, the plant
that does not grow in exile's walkways.
　　My father, who knew this city's every twist,
had mapped the heart's closed-in terrain —
　　had accounted for each stored grievance
hidden in the mind's cellar under weighty fear.
　　I am his will manifest: his way to step once more
in time, and take up arms in the world of flesh.
　　Had I resentments, they were ground to salt.

Morning returned without notice — pressing down
　　like earth on the back of a buried man.
The window showed a sky littered with clouds
　　with wind a diversion, yet still not dispersing —
and all the time a dull thud in my neck.
　　Indeed we'd arrived, each for a reason.
Get your things on, follow me out, you already
　　had your trousers on, your back disguised

in the wave of your shirt. *It's time.* Indeed it was—
    and through the dark of it, I never once doubted
the truth of your words—though in convalescence
    I can still wonder whether it was fear
or the crowd that sounded like thunder.

TRIESTE

Night comes in on its hands and knees.
Outside, somewhere, a wave breaks on a word.
Lovers begin their distance run.
Night in its shadow is a bystander;
a vanquished man.

The moon is seldom full. In Trieste, Joyce still walks,
an impassioned man, bearing his one good eye.
The shore beats back its own pulse.
Roofs sigh. Men hitch up their pants,
leave without a sound.

Night hoists its bags and continues, there is always a later train.

TRAINS AT NIGHT

I

The train's shadowy corridor is an apology:
a winding argument of thrusts and retreats,
whose odd logic keeps the night
navigator pinned by turns to the window's
reflection, or cast up against compartments

where the tremulous sleep, under a blanket
of half-closed eyes. One can no longer
examine a book under the light, nor grasp
what towns, distant as islands, signal
back regarding their neglect or survival.

II

At L., boarding the train with companions,
the countryside evolved strange and fallow,
finally sinking back like a man in water.
In the tide of that grey-green hour,
we held to our seats like stone promontories,

drifted in sleep, the sleep before rain,
waking as if threatened by waves of a northern sea.
Then there were diversions, and the melancholy
of distance. The canopy of baggage revealed
in time: oranges, a bit of chocolate for the weary.

III

Midnight stop. Sleep undone by paradox:
stillness wakes. Past filmed windows an
initiate boards, the goodbye short, the ascension
swift. There will be voices in the corridor.
An arrangement of seats. Whistles.

In the dim compartment heavy with breath
a watch is held to the pale station light.
Somewhere off a man raises his hand, calling
into the dark with a practiced motion.
The train starts into its longest tunnel.

IV

Here, do we dream of the intricate nature
of seasons, or of loss, which suddenly catches us
up short, among strangers whose breathing
makes us long for the familiar entities:
faded geometrics on bedroom paper,

ceilings whose cracks lead us out to gardens,
where our sorrows are trimmed privately
as the roses we keep, where the occasional bird
chooses to visit without invitation,
and with no intention of staying on.

V

The corridor, a refuge for the late-night smokers,
sees itself mirrored as it rounds a bend:
steady as a figure, blade to ice.
Within, its low lights are comfort and confidant —
soothing those who tread softly in their rounds;

pacing out night's invisible path, they will
be found first in the morning at the door's release.
For now a window drawn down must suffice:
night air comes in startling as Pandora's triumph,
the great rush of wind, the intelligible terror.

VI

The door slides open at the border. The barnyards
are in shadow, the patrolmen edgy: the searches.
Further down the train, each piece of luggage is checked.
Language, formal, reveals little.
A bit of fear chases the throat dry as a wrapped parcel.

Then it is night again, faces disrupted by
their own gravity. Breathing the bridge
between memory and knowledge. Lying in the dark
there is nothing but time, it waits beside you
until the first tug of steam, the discernable forward motion.

II

The Art of Measuring Light

THE ART OF MEASURING LIGHT

From the Pont-Neuf, Paris

The light here has begun to pass and as it passes
it will bend down to the Seine in the last of its
winter gymnastics: unwrapping its hands from
the white crevices of Saint-Germain-des-Prés,

giving a last honor to Sacré-Cœur. One will
turn one's eyes to the horizon, but there only
shadows lie, and the beams of cars that follow
the Seine northward toward Le Havre, their lamps

yellow like the pleasure boats that illuminate
the shores with serpentine eyes. But standing
in half-light, the mind devises a method,
and knows that distance is an arc, not a line;

it will follow light as it curves past the river
to meet its welcome in woods, distant from
the sphere of the thinker, yet distant only as
a pair of hands, clasping a tool in a far-off field.

The body in its accuracy cannot close the calipers
of space, but knows just the same that light
that has passed here is light that will contrive
to touch the white of wood on maple-lined streets,

deep in New Hampshire, where snow is piling
high, in the unbroken shadow of a new day.
Where for the difference of six hours, the hands
of the clock are unlocked, and Puritans progress

with morning. They will carve out a day, wrapped
in time, envisaged in the silence of apple and pine,
and of light curving to where it will break in the
suddenness of a windfall. Perhaps there one will

measure a quantum leap, where from pasture post,
to the end of the road, light will seize the form
of an animal breathless beneath the carcass
of a rusted frame; or watch as it breaks stride

at crossroads, finding figures passing surrounded
by the wreath of their breath. The sky is not a narrow
passage, and light is there to flex the ample arm of it.
On this side, the Pont-Neuf is dark, and the mind,

that lone traveler, comes back to rest like a cast
shuttle to a waiting palm. Across the bridges
night figures come, their loads weighted like
lanterns — swinging slowly in narrow arcs.

THE BODY IN YOUTH

After rain, in the darkened room, the body
reed-like, marked by mysteries, hungered
to escape the rhythm of change, observed
nightly in the narrow bed.

Shadowless, the washed walls receded,
though benignly, in triptych, caught the
occasional beam's passing: such
the simple Annunciations

that taught limbs to reach, as if in passion,
into the near vagaries of space. Each part
resolutely delivered its tidings: ears
fanned and thickened like

muscular flowers, that thrive in the shade
of the water's edge; birthmarks, hidden,
spread, then darkened, inspected by fingers
for their singular shape.

Ribs betrayed the pulse's quickening pace.
Only dreams cradled imperfections —
rationalized the humidity of desires;
by day the body crept

to the mirror and under its scrutiny,
waited for change like an unseen horizon.
Just before rain it seemed the body
lingered transparent,

had carried one out under the firs, set
one free under the rotating spheres.
Now flesh was a constant breath
at one's ear, intoning

its litany of limitations. Yet how far the body
had to travel — when finally, after its shape
was fixed, and became one's signature
in the world of forms,

then faithlessly, like a ship tide-persuaded,
it drifted, abandoning what it sought
to become, the body in youth lingering
only a moment in its own folds.

DIPTYCH

For Glenn
Patrick Llompart, 1956–1991

I. Pietà

The bed where you once lay together
had become a cross, and those thin feet
at its base seemed not to touch the linen.

His great eyes watched you so, until
on the wing of their own death, they retreated,
his voice following, muted by solitude.

At night you lifted him on your lap, then to
the toilet — to the window, to let some last
image enter his eyes. You were no longer lover

but witness then, and watched as his body
followed its slow journey toward a horizon
of shades and gathering stillness.

Then, it happened: his garden called
him, and the desire to walk where
the last leaves moved, and the twisted

cypress trees of his youth spoke. By then
he was beyond grief, and only your own
left you at his feet, prostrate.

II. *Arranging the Garments*

You left him there in a stony place,
but carried his voice in your hearing
as dew stays in a land snail's shell.

Afterwards, in familiar rooms,
there were the garments by the bed
the ones that had held his form,

until this too was gone. You take one
to the window, and under its paleness
the warp is lost, and folded there

in your hands, it lies like a brow
released of a final thought. Nothing
will again animate the sleeve or neck,

nothing will soften the collar's cut
the way the head turning at a window did.
The garments wait like the dead —

In a final rite your body stoops
and speaks to that one now no longer
of the place, and you hold another

piece to the light, as if this time his
shape might come, but it does not.
Slowly you turn to arrange the lot.

PARABLE OF THE LOVERS

That summer made a fool of the darkness.
Under the branches of trees, animals carried on.

The bees stayed at work in their hives.
Water flowed intently, as at sunrise.

And intruders fell mute as they walked through
the glowing landscape, able to hear foxes

in the earth, and the sound of nesting birds.
The sky was filled with many strange shapes.

Planets rushed through the brief night and
meteors spelled out their language in long

thin strokes. Only lovers failed to detect
the strangeness of the solstice, so innocent

were they of time. Above, in the cypresses,
the cicadas' chant sought their hearing,

but it was lost to them as the water wove
again its star-filled current:

You two who wander in the violet dark,
leaving the taste of wild sage on one another's

mouth, when you part, the other's body will
reside in yours like salt in the earth.

You will learn that longing is the origin of exile
and unreconciled to grief, you will know

that there where you lay, under the chestnut's
wide hand, listening to the wild owls —

the angel hung over you.

ON A VISIT TO BUDAPEST

One cannot live without love — this statement
so simple, so mundane, came to me in that
city where we roamed around the baths. I
hadn't known it until the tilt of your head,
suddenly, in shadow, confirmed all I knew,
and though my children and husband waited
I let you lay me down while the wind berated
the dry leaves overhead. What I hadn't
known was how, at forty, the heart can
reanimate — and how plans, even one's
own flesh, can drift, suddenly out of focus,
seen from the wrong end of a telescope.
When I returned, my husband hadn't noticed.
The children looked up from their play
murmuring their own eccentricities,
I thought about you night and day, until
it seemed I would burst with words unsaid,
unraged. Daylight transfigured all I knew.
Every motion seemed absurd — clothes
packed in trunks seemed like funeral chests
where once I lay down and gave myself away.
I'm not the same as I was at twenty-two,
yet once I was glad to walk the streets
at night and listen to how dawn would light
on my sill. I hear it still, but before today it
was the far-off echo of a voice faded
behind a wall, distance claiming its toll.
If life is hazardous, this the greatest one of all:
the heart cannot be led like a dog
but rises up, and seeks its goal.

FANTASIE ON *THE CHURCH AT AUVERS*

After Van Gogh

At ten o'clock the light gives out, and although
something remains — luminous as a voice — in
the distance the trees are monochrome, a line
of black, querulous as archaic speech.

We walk here patterning our talk at intervals,
to stop where the last light hovers, secular
and mad, in a clearing sky. Our words, like
the sound of paper, or the low lull

of water at the water's edge, would have failed
to register in his formal handling of oil and we,
passersby, would have been silent if caught in
his brush at twilight, passing the forbidding

church, planted among low brush and crowding
cypress. To paint though, is to render surfaces —
and so, while we walk, we talk of the dimmed
and winding spirals that lead back

to early memory, plaintively set in landscapes
of less elliptical light. Perhaps his reasons
physiological, epilepsy fashioning the rhythm
of motion within the cells, while we,

condemned to plainer madness, recall the curve
of the figure that held the lock, or the silhouette,
which remained statuesque, never rendering
speech into the midst of our gathering

absence. We lose and loosen such things on our
way, yet, caught, we would have been a pair —
darkness spreading its hands on us, as we came
to regard the bent, shadowy painter

mapping the curves of twilight's evensong.

III
The Jumping Figure

THE STAIRWELL, BERGGASSE 19,
VIENNA

*From 1891 to 1938, Berggasse 19 was the location
of Freud's consulting rooms and, one flight above, his
private quarters. On March 15, 1938, the house-
hold was invaded by Brownshirts. In June of the
same year, the Freuds left Austria for England.*

I

The stairwell bore the weight of their visits —
those who each day came, and climbed
to the green door with its marble lintel;
they paused there, like water drawn up

from a source, before the knock. Then an eye
to the eyepiece — the doctor's entryway
with hat and cape. The waiting room pure
bourgeoisie. Where, with small

> *Dreams are disconnected, they accept*
> *the most violent contradictions without*
> *the least objection . . .*

movements of hands and feet, they
would wait to enter the idol-heavy dark.
Left behind, in the corner, a box of cards,
with images like those that later

came to mind: an acrobat whose skirt is
blown like the skin of glass around a lamp,
and the man whose fingers clutch
laurel as if in drowning hands.

they admit impossibilities, they disregard
knowledge which carries great weight with
us in the daytime . . .

Pausing after, on the stair, a hand would grasp
the simple rail, and wonder how the branches
bent beyond the inlaid window's frame.
And he, day-work

done, would climb the stair, collar in hand
to where the hearth's warmth flickered.
But even as dream-forms in the night
came clear to him,

Faustian elements gathered force,
massed like dark water under bridges;
thirsty as the primal horde, they bent
together and lit their torches.

As in dreams . . . in a group the function for
testing the reality of things falls into the
background in comparison with the
strength of willful impulses . . .

II

An individual immersed for some time in
a group soon finds himself . . . in a special
state, which resembles the state of
"fascination", in which the hypnotized
individual finds himself in the hands of
the hypnotizer . . .

Tonight, in a silence edged with passersby,
memory delivers back that particular cast
of twilight when brown-shirted figures climbed
the stairs. Their heels, like

spades on the floor, crushed the inlaid flowers
underneath. Then the lapse before the knock
that disturbed the sleep of all Vienna.
But it was natural

to let the visitor in, natural to use the daily set
of words: *Meine Herren, wie geht's uns denn*
heute abend? while life's common
backdrop revealed

itself as a state of grace. Through the shifting
silt of fear knowledge fragmented then
coalesced — here new threats borrowed
from ancient tongues,

repeating the well-known litany: *The enemy
said, 'I will pursue, I will overtake — my desire
shall have its fill of them'*. Finally,
given money, the hypnotized

retreated, the stairs carrying their young
bodies down like rusted water
draining from a shed.

> *In a group the individual is allowed to throw off
> the repression of his unconscious instinctual
> impulses. The apparently new characteristics are
> in fact manifestations of this unconscious in
> which all that is evil in the human mind is
> contained as a predisposition.*

The hand was already

on the lock. He turned: the Gypsy in the box
hung upside-down, the eagle above the lovers
grimly held its prey. By what distress
did he again open the door,

finally prepared for flight, his exodus
beginning with the marble extending, this time
its softest hand — as down he went, following
the balustrade's ebony path.

NIGHT IN CLAMART

Marina Tsvetayeva, 1933

As if the first night,
hyacinths are speaking
color to the darkness.

As when you walked,
head down, head hung
with stars,

along roads written
as afterthoughts,
threatened with dissolution

by dirty rains.
Contretemps your lot,
passion its antidote.

The empty roads
tonight look
for your shadow,

but you are neither
form nor voice,
unable to describe

their makeshift rifts,
their part in the joke
loss and circumstance

played on you. If one
could call to you tonight!
Tell you it's all beginning,

the rivers starting again
from their sources, your
native homes, Moscow,

Prague, moving like
bridge ice into water. *
For a moment there

is laughter, and the
moon rises like a kite
on its narrow string.

Only time betrayed
you, gutting you of
all you had, making you

ring out your sorrowful
notes, in the dark of night
and with no goodbye.

FROM: *THE SEVEN WONDERS OF THE MODERN WORLD*

Things that have vanished remain:
as mysteries, wonders and terrors.

August 13, 1961, Berlin

As if without notice, it began: curls of wire
emerging from warehouse depths, engendering
a darkness that gathered like a storm

in the distance. Still, when morning came,
and the barrier with it, there was a moment
when even the doers were caught unawares.

And as if at low tide, one could still step,
and wade across morning and the mounting wire,
one's glasses in one's hand. But not for long:

the barrier was suddenly a net pulled taut,
a breakwater that bodies could not cross,
and daylight was halved like a pear,

divided for the two sides of the identical street,
each knowing its abandoned twin, its other
pulse. How had consciousness arrived that day,

what dreams of open spaces were harbored in
the last moments, before the soul would turn
and see it was only staring in the mirror;

neither Hadrian, nor the dynasties, had equal
resources to build a wall this impenetrable.
Cordoned within the concrete hedge, each

man became a Dædalus heating his wax;
or, more pedestrian — the circus feat: a leap
from a window while the police climbed

the stairs. The ancient gods remark: how
ingenious to change the nature of distance
itself — a mile can take a lifetime to traverse.

So when flight was lost, or the ordinary
movement across open space, time too was captured,
held back like a clock in a drawer, possibility

suddenly a figure whose voice in the distance
resisted understanding. Tongues had been separated,
one from the other, to keep the spiraling tower

from growing, but here the same tongue, the same
voice was parted, one side quartered like a figure
in a shuttered room. How ingenious, say the gods,

to take that which is the same, and leave part
to grow like a bud that is season-touched, while
the other is left to form like fruit in a bottle.

THE ROMAN ARBOR

Suddenly you felt it. And under the white
eye of afternoon, you turned

but could see nothing. Water flowed from
the mouths of the stone heads,

that hung, as if sacrificed, above their basins
in the trellised garden. You caught,

in an alcove of green, the quick movement
of a lizard as it traced the sandal

of a departed goddess. The garden was so still
that, apart from the shifting water,

you imagined sound had refused refuge there,
preferring to venture out towards

where the islands broke the authority of the
shoreline. Your calm was restored.

So when you met, face to face between the
columns, you were not prepared —

he stood greater than you, his stone locks
worn smooth as the tide's back,

his breast four times the hand's compass.
Breathless before his bulk, you

failed to notice that afternoon was gaining
territory. Then, slowly, under

the heat, a thought crept along the stone sills,
leaving behind a thin trail of grief.

Who is not like him — you asked — your words
sifting in the striated light,

and turning as the sand lifted once in
the hot breeze, you said:

Who is not a witness of ruined places?

PLANISFÉRIA, MAP OF THE WORLD, LISBON, 1554

Space was easier then, and time slower —
One faced the white of distance with purpose.
    The unknown beckoned, like the polar caps,
      or stilled one, like an awkward moment:

beyond the horizon, trees stirred like birds;
heedless of latitude, temperatures rose,
    fir trees bent, their needles uncalculated.
    This desire to possess, to flatten space

was dwarfed by waves that the astrolabe could
not settle. Yet, the mapmaker took sides:
    Africa would be veined with great water
    arteries, but the Amazon would diminish

halfway across the *Mundus Novus*.
Other rivers were silenced, though needed:
    to be known, land must be entered
    by those green arched passageways

above which birds in formal plumage
led the way to inland knowledge. Still,
    whole continents slid off: passed up and cast
    into the corner of the mapmaker's dark.

DEATH OF THE TYRANT

One day, like hard October frost, he came to them,
though it took time for each to adapt.

Sour-faced drummers rattled their sticks in the square,
  while the birds left their nests, darkening
  the sky with their departure.

  Grains hardened on the staff.

The city soon sagged under the weight of days.
Passion and language were bent on the wheel:

seasons held down by the hand of function
  bore neither fruit nor folly. The tyrant
  was familiar by then,

  a family man.

He could be seen walking his dogs on Sunday
afternoons. And each January he let flow

a black ribbon of words from the podium.
  Since the hourglass had been destroyed,
  time ceased. At night

  there was a strange

calm, and all the animals that might have
bayed, one day simply disappeared —

followed by fountain pens, handkerchiefs,
  and bread.
  Dawn was grey as cement.

  But silent as rust breeding

came the day when the south wind picked up
the paper in its mouth.

The soup suddenly boiled on the stoves.
        And bodies in uniform floated
        down the river like light barges.

    Once again sundials

cast their angles, and though silent,
the birds returned

perching above the castle like sentinels.
        A fire flared and the flames
        spoke in tongues.

    Seized with anxiety,

the city awaited the news. But after
the white bodies of saints had

risen from their graves, some secretly
        wept. Morning had cleared
        their downcast eyes, accustomed

    so long to partial sight:

their city, which once boasted gold-faced
towers, cerulean-tipped flowers and

resplendent leaves — now lay before them
        like abolished tender, and they
        stared like those before

    the gates of hell.

THE JUMPING FIGURE

*After months of public assurance that there would be
no barrier built between East and West Berlin, on
the morning of August 13, 1961, the first barbed
wire was erected; in the following weeks, doors and
windows of apartments facing West Berlin were sealed.*

All day I have heard the sirens calling,
confiding to the distance a suffering
which moves each moment closer. Here among
familiar things, I hesitate before
my task: I am the figure in the clock
that hourly appears on the ledge, then
retreats from that beleaguered edge into
the close and shuttered dark. If I falter
it's that the past holds me so, in these rooms
where each night I have laid my
head — fatigued by choices I didn't make —
on linen white and neatly kept, yet soiled
by dreams of those once left for dead along
the routes that greatness took. And now as if
again disgraced, tanks move slowly through the
dust that's had barely fifteen years to rest.
Patience had been my guiding star. But can
I say I didn't choose to feel a certain
ecstasy in that first, long-ago spring, or feel
my girlhood bloom under the voices of furious
power? Then, when life was out of doors, one
waited in white under the linden trees,
as if the future too would arrive, swept
with the rest down the avenue.

                                        Now I'm

fitted like a fixture in this room.

After the war, the days that followed
seemed like time scattered on barren ground —
I walked alone bereft, as light cut through
the buildings with mirages. I was nineteen.
The year that might have been my glory
I passed bricks hand over hand, and watched
as birds rose from the ruins. So dreadful were
the deprivations, as the clouds moved in
vague formations, one almost hoped therein
for some redemption. Today, again displaced,
as if my body has been pledged to a dynasty
perched a third time on the edge:
I am left to survey the fall.

But why

think now of such things? It's just that faces
in this room profess a perfect innocence —
the photographs lean in like a pious chorus
exacting these ultimate confessions.
Below a crowd stretches a cloth, as if
to define the territory of my absolution.

I know

I have not grasped the nature of things,
but remember how velocity adds its hand
to that which drops from a height —
and know enough to fear the peace of those
who've missed the net: for as their faces
were free, their limbs were grasped
in such calligrams of despair. Through
my door I hear the sounds of those
who've come to seal my fate; held still by
the hands of doubt, I've let my body lean out:
I must accept the path my feet dictate.

IV

The Idiom of the Place

PAULA MODERSOHN-BECKER
AT WORPSWEDE

Paula Modersohn-Becker began her career as a
painter in the small German art colony of
Worpswede. In an attempt to break with the
prevailing visual idiom there, she made four trips to
Paris, the last in 1906. She died following childbirth
after returning to her husband in Worpswede.

Each morning, from the same palette
the landlocked hamlet came to light.
Night had sketched the shadowy forms,
and from its traces, birches, brave white,

issued forth their lines, laced the canal's
sinuous path. You began here: this marsh
the ground of your colors; you faced
the unlanguagable green of firs, drew

the uncombed bank alight. Evening saw
your reflection bend in the paleness
at the water's edge, and pass where piled
peat rose, darkened like temples after

sudden rain. You loved the idiom
of the place. But as a foot cannot retrace
its step in ground grown cold
since its passing, so repetitions bear

their weight on one who takes them
on day after day: a palette like a landscape
can grow too small, and fade, failing
to tell how noon lay bright or fallow,

or how it turned pressed on by imagination's
weight. Suddenly, color may turn unforgiving
and fail you in even another word.
So when something strange, almost southern

seized you in your bones, your *Landschaft*
could not bear up under a red that
seemed to speak in tongues, and a pink
that rose up, an island, untamed.

Even rendering your own form betrayed
your need to penetrate to the heart: any vanity
was left behind to see yourself in the mirror
as the mirror sees itself. Could the pain

of losing homeland compare with this:
to see daylight, finally, over the Seine,
and Cézanne's colors found in a gallery —
you gave up twilight, the pastoral figure

in half-light, to pass into knowing.
Death would come uneasily, calling out
your name with regret. You who had come
so close to color at the moment's edge.

MUNCH IN OSLO

Photographic portrait, 1902

You've removed your shoes,
that in the thin gaslight might
take on some different shape,

in the blank moment when
thought is equal to silence,
and even memory hangs at

bay, waiting for a moment
of greater waking.
Then you straighten

yourself on the bed, which
gives a little, with a sigh,
and survey the ceiling.

The paintings do not speak.
They are shadows in the other
room, all imperfect.

The molding arches darken
like January on a medieval calendar.
The doors aspirate, pull

and release on their hinges,
and Oslo's cold fastens itself
to the window. A bucket forms

a small dark lake on the floor, and
bottles sit as on a chemist's
shelf. In the moment of dark

there still is time, and not time
enough. The heater's pagoda
warms the air, now silver-still.

READING

You are committed to living in the open,
but today somehow the timbers of the city,
rustic and baroque, complicate an already

oppressive sky. Inside a gentler light hangs
over you — a mother. You read, marking
pages with the slight moisture of your hand,

pressing the leaves between fingers,
as your eyes scan the lines. Outside there
is no sign of change. Tourists like bands

of thieves continue on their regular routes,
making the air sting with intermittent
exchange. Time is a facsimile of itself.

You watch from the window as an old man
passes again, for the fourth time, making
his way along the long hollow of the day.

Your book left on its spine is a bird in flight.
Later, the dark settles in, a far-off motion.
At night you dream fall in its yellow

acridness arrives — at the market you
fill your basket with apples, the harvest
of native fruits, the weeping hand of dill.

WAKING AT NIGHT

Frightened, pulled from an awkward depth,
we wait as time and place spin in the near dark.
Your body once unbounded in sleep, tempered,
now shifts like a coracle tied. You reach for me

where I settle on the edge of an even beat,
a landing in a distant landscape.
Once lifted, your head, drawn in shadow,
gathers the light that lingers in corners,

your eyes, at odds with the imperial dark,
are eager to prove the rationality of a tiny room.
Yet fear remains and tenaciously so,
seated at the bottom of this half-finished night,

stubborn as a stone mired in a watery depth
immovable by hands or the tide's incessant flow.
We are always homeless in these longest hours.
You will wait for day to cross the yard —

to answer the need your eyes betray,
their surface mottled as a darkening fire.
Reflection on the hour, breath held in, exhaled —
for you the shadow of time draws close.

Suddenly a light angles a path, touching
our room with its translucent cast.
Finally, perhaps day has come — your mouth
forms a sentence, as if this visitation

could make some reparation with your past
that turns like a helix in the dark.
But transient, fugitive, light is gone
before you could memorize just what it showed;

The neighbor, you say in a rusty voice —
equal to us in this nocturnal anticipation.
Your breath soon misty, exhales by memory
a few of the milky, salvaged scenes;

yet as you beg toward the wall to let yourself out —
a dory released to drift on the moonlit tide,
your mind in ambulation asks if the fear was not real,
finding expression in these inland waters.

PHOTOGRAPH, OFF THE DRY SALVAGES

In a photograph of him in his younger
years, before his hair had become dark
and thin, before his face had developed
its regal set — one can glimpse still, immobile
eyes that had not yet seen his death,
in the coming of a tide, coming in combed
in white, had not yet seen the garden
with the pool, and the ghostly images
that floated there — still young, his head
crowned in thought, his profile soft,
one can sense yet the intensity of his talk —
of love perhaps, his own voice sweet
as the hyacinth girl that struck him speechless
on the street.

THE SERMON TO FISHES

He was struck with awe at the sight of them:
a shoal lifting above the water's surface;
each head trained to his voice's timbre,
each spine anchored for the moment's purpose.

For the sea-dark flock, he fixed his words,
he the shepherd above them.
In the distance the itinerant waves obeyed
by ritual motion. Words flew from him —

How he had rehearsed such a miracle!
Before the silver of their scales, and
the heads in seeming infinite number,
he was great and gathered them in his hunger.

Yet, once lulled, how quiet this multitude —
that like quarter notes broke the water's line
as if hovering above the stillness where the lowest
staff separates music from endless silence.

Though his words had touched their hearing
and their heads above the water were tamed
he was pinned by his eye in water.
Arms outstretched, his figure remained

rooted, and would never master what, in one
movement turning round, they did, descending
guiltless into water, which glimmered darkly
as they fanned out, flying downward.

TONES OVERHEARD ON MONASTERY GROUNDS

Sound penetrates, holds in the distance. And then —
the intermittent brush of April against the transept.
We listen. A child's voice fades through a back door
like day through a velvet cloth. This, a rhythmic

motif that will never be heard again, ever. And these:
chance light, sound, the movement of bodies,
are joined for a moment like the final section
of a symphony heard only once, and then, in sleep.

Adagio. Slowly this perfection modulates like color
warming and cooling through its spectrum of hues.
But what is lost? Do these rhythms, these accidental
variations attach themselves to candlesticks,

or the base of a lone saint, worm-eaten, in his own
way a beggar of time? Will the resonances last,
will they stay in the form of a shadow, so carefully
laid, a stranger will be able to read our passing?

And what of the moments in another's presence —
do words, like intermittent vibrations, register
in the mind, like weather not to be repeated,
a sentence penetrating like a ray through clouds

above monastery grounds, angling in such a way
it seems it will never again fall so? Or a glance,
suddenly so true, mimicking the green of a branch
by an ancient door, so specific, it seems an Epiphany?

Much is lost. Even these exchanges that make
the heart rise, dissolve like light on weathered ground
that humbles and exalts. Yet as day's hand caresses
again the forlorn saint, so too are we changed:

the touch of time stays with us as we look.

CANTICLE IN GREY

For Anna Akhmatova

And I can't return! But even beyond Lethe I will take with me
The living outlines of my gardens at Tsarskoye Selo
A. A.

The bridges over the Neva bear the touch
      of dusk, and slowly the river makes its trail
            through mist — a web undone at night by rain.
Can we continue to act, despite all. This you
      asked — as now your voice penetrates this dark,
            where once you sat alone on evening's shore.

On the same sea where Ovid walked the shore
      of exile, you were born: your brow bore the noble touch
            of the ancient calendar. Before evening's dark
you could walk along the verdant summer trail
      gathering sounds: never knowing that for you
            lay a sorrow of home equal to exile's reign.

Still, there was time. At Tsarskoye Selo, in the rain,
      you listened for your master along allées by the shore
            where he had passed. Among the gardens you
learned your craft. And if your eyes could still touch
      the golden spires, or swan's legs in flight left to trail,
            in dreams you heard the sound of an impending dark.

And when the sky filled with a ravening dark
        you stood, watched as the present dissolved as rain
                draws still green leaves to the ground — a trail
of deaths passed by your door. Now an invisible shore
        separated you from the past — and your voice's touch,
                like Cassandra's above the war, found only you.

St. Petersburg was sunk as below a tide. Alone you
        watched it while your double, your intimate dark
                life that couldn't be, still roamed — went on to touch
what should have been: lovers hidden from the rain,
        the inventions of spring along the familiar shore —
                while your body's shadow followed its given trail.

Winter again: beneath frost's hand a spiraling trail
        of bodies held to relentless queues. Undaunted, you
                stayed, as the prison wall like a sightless shore
cast up its victims in the snow. And through the dark
        you remained — a bronze figure softened by rain
                who above a broken jug could praise the water's touch.

Here, by the shore, figures pass slowly in the dark,
        their thoughts trail like willow branches in the rain.
                They stop. Is it you? Silently the updraft's touch.

NOTES

"March 26, 1827"
"The singer Lablanche, seeking news of Beethoven, arrived to find him
in a coma, delirious, and could make out but these few words: 'do you
hear the tolling? Change the scene . . .' It could not, in this context, per-
tain to anything but the bells in the theaters of Vienna that, during this
period, announced the changing of the acts." See Jean and Brigitte Mas-
sin, *Ludwig van Beethoven* (Paris: Fayard, 1967), 494.

"Lebensraum"
Literally, "living space"; the name for Hitler's policy of acquiring enough
land to create a nation of two hundred million German people.

"The temple of Janus": Janus was one of the principal Roman gods. His
shrine in the Forum in Rome had two doors, which were closed in times
of peace and open in times of war. He is represented as having two faces,
looking in opposite directions; these symbolize his ability to see both the
future and the past.

"Standards rising in the eagle's shadow": A symbol used by the Roman mili-
tary, the eagle also adorned Nazi military standards.

"The fallen Polish cavalry": The cavalry, used since ancient times, was still
viewed by many at the outbreak of the Second World War as a viable form
of military strength. In 1939, the impressive Polish cavalry rode out to re-
pel the invading panzers: "In a few minutes . . . the cavalry lay in a smok-
ing, screaming mass of dismembered and disemboweled men and horses."
Paul Fussell, *Wartime* (New York: Oxford University Press, 1989), 5.

"The Stairwell, Berggasse 19, Vienna"
One of history's most famous addresses, Berggasse 19 was the site of
Freud's consulting rooms and, one flight above, his living quarters. Freud
left Austria in 1938; he died the following year in London.

"Dreams are disconnected, they admit . . . in the daytime": Sigmund Freud,
The Interpretation of Dreams (New York: Avon Books, 1965), 87.

"As in dreams": Sigmund Freud, "Group Psychology and the Analysis of
the Ego," in *Civilization, Society and Religion* (London: Penguin Books,
1985), 108.

"An individual immersed": G. Le Bon, *Psychologie des foules* (Paris, 1895), as quoted in Freud, "Group Psychology and the Analysis of the Ego," 102.

"But it is natural": The Freuds' sangfroid during the March 15 raid was described thus by their son Martin: "[Martha Freud] treated them as ordinary visitors, inviting them to put their rifles down in the sections of the hall-stand reserved for umbrellas, and even to sit down. . . . Father too had retained his invincible poise, leaving his sofa where he had been resting to join Mother in the living room where he sat calmly in his armchair throughout the raid." *The Diary of Sigmund Freud 1929–1939*, edited by Michael Molnar (London: Hogarth Press, 1992).

"The enemy said": Exodus 15:9.

"In a group the individual": Freud, "Group Psychology and the Analysis of the Ego," 101.

"Night in Clamart"
The Russian poet Marina Tsvetayeva lived briefly in the Parisian suburb of Petit Clamart during her exile from the Soviet Union, 1922–39. She returned to the Soviet Union in 1939. In 1941, under harsh government reprisals, she committed suicide.

"From: *The Seven Wonders of the Modern World*"
Originally a list of the most remarkable structures of the ancient world as set down in about 200 B.C., the seven wonders of the ancient world included the Pyramid of Khufu, the Hanging Gardens of Babylon, the Statue of Zeus at Olympia, the Temple of Diana at Ephesus, the Mausoleum at Halicarnassus, the Colossus of Rhodes, and the Lighthouse of Alexandria. Since then, similar lists have been compiled by various ages.

"And as if at low tide": "A middle-aged East Berlin couple, having only learned of the night's developments at 9:00 that morning, went down to see for themselves. Spotting a stretch of wire barrier that was still incomplete and, for the moment, unguarded, the man said to his wife, '*Hop oder top*' ('Now or never'), and across they went." Norman Gelb, *The Berlin Wall* (New York: Simon and Schuster, 1986), 174.

"Cordoned within": Dædalus, commissioned to build a labyrinth for Queen Pasiphae of Crete, "found himself imprisoned there too. . . . To escape from the prison he had made himself, Dædalus constructed two pairs of wings on which he and Icarus flew away from Crete." Michael Stapleton, *A Dictionary of Greek and Roman Mythology* (New York: Bell Publishing Company, 1978), 60.

68

"Canticle in Grey"

Though persecuted by the Soviet government after the Revolution, the Russian poet Anna Akhmatova, a contemporary of Marina Tsvetayeva, remained in the Soviet Union as a witness to the atrocities of the Stalinist period.

"Where Ovid walked the shore": Ovid was exiled from Rome in 8 A.D. and lived out his final years on the Black Sea. Akhmatova was born in 1889 on the Black Sea.

"Tsarskoye Selo": The summer residence of the Russian royal family where Akhmatova spent her first sixteen years.

"For your master": Tsarskoye Selo is also associated with Pushkin, who attended the lyceum there as a boy.

"Prison wall": Among the many forms of intimidation that Akhmatova suffered under Stalin was the near-constant incarceration of her son.